LET'S COOK WITH
Eggs!

Delicious & Fun Egg Dishes Kids Can Make

Nancy Tuminelly

Consulting Editor, Diane Craig, M.A./Reading Specialist

A Division of ABDO
ABDO
Publishing Company

visit us at www.abdopublishing.com

Published by ABDO Publishing Company, a division of ABDO, P.O. Box 398166, Minneapolis, Minnesota 55439. Copyright © 2013 by Abdo Consulting Group, Inc. International copyrights reserved in all countries. No part of this book may be reproduced in any form without written permission from the publisher. Super SandCastle™ is a trademark and logo of ABDO Publishing Company.

Printed in the United States of America, North Mankato, Minnesota
062012
092012

 PRINTED ON RECYCLED PAPER

Editor: Liz Salzmann
Content Developer: Nancy Tuminelly
Cover and Interior Design and Production: Colleen Dolphin, Mighty Media, Inc.
Food Production: Desirée Bussiere
Photo Credits: Colleen Dolphin, Shutterstock, iStockphoto (Gary Milner, Dawna Stafford)

The following manufacturers/names appearing in this book are trademarks: Clear Value® Taco Seasoning, Contadina® Pizza Sauce, Green Giant® Cream Style Sweet Corn, Hellman's® Real Mayonnaise, Market Pantry® Pure Vanilla Extract, McCormick® Imitation Almond Extract, McCormick® Pure Mint Extract, Morton® Iodized Salt, PAM® Baking Spray, Proctor Silex® Hand Blender, Pyrex® Measuring Glass, Roundy's® Distilled White Vinegar, Simply Potatoes® Shredded Hash Browns

Library of Congress Cataloging-in-Publication Data
Tuminelly, Nancy, 1952-
  Let's cook with eggs! : delicious & fun egg dishes kids can make / Nancy Tuminelly.
    p. cm. -- (Super simple recipes)
  Audience: Ages 4-10.
  ISBN 978-1-61783-421-9
  1. Cooking (Eggs)--Juvenile literature. 2. Quick and easy cooking--Juvenile literature. 3. Cookbooks. I. Title.
  TX745.T86 2013
  641.6'75--dc23
                        2011052196

Super SandCastle™ books are created by a team of professional educators, reading specialists, and content developers around five essential components—phonemic awareness, phonics, vocabulary, text comprehension, and fluency—to assist young readers as they develop reading skills and strategies and increase their general knowledge. All books are written, reviewed, and leveled for guided reading, early reading intervention, and Accelerated Reader® programs for use in shared, guided, and independent reading and writing activities to support a balanced approach to literacy instruction.

Note to Adult Helpers

Helping kids learn how to cook is fun! It's a great way to practice math and science. Cooking teaches kids about responsibility and boosts their confidence. Plus, they learn how to help out in the kitchen! The recipes in this book require adult assistance. Make sure there is always an adult around when kids are in the kitchen. Expect kids to make a mess, but also expect them to clean up after themselves. Most importantly, make the experience pleasurable by sharing and enjoying the food kids make.

Symbols

Knife
Always ask an adult to help you use knives.

Microwave
Be careful with hot food! Learn more on page 7.

Oven
Have an adult help put things into and take them out of the oven. Learn more on page 7.

Stovetop
Be careful around hot burners! Learn more on page 7.

Contents

Let's Cook with Eggs!

People have been eating eggs pretty much since people first existed! At first they took eggs from the nests of wild birds. Birds were first raised for eggs in Asia and India. This was more than 5,000 years ago! Now people all over the world eat eggs.

Most of the eggs people eat come from chickens. A hen can lay about 250 eggs a year. Eggs come in different colors and sizes. The color of the **yolk** depends on what the chicken eats.

Eggs are good for you. They have **protein**, **vitamins**, and **minerals**. These things make your body grow strong. There are many ways to cook with eggs.

The recipes in this book are simple. It's fun using one main ingredient! Cooking teaches you about food, measuring, and following directions. Enjoy your tasty treats with your family and friends!

Think Safety!

- Ask an adult to help you use knives. Use a cutting board.

- Clean up spills to prevent accidents.

- Keep tools and **utensils** away from the edge of the table or counter.

- Use a step stool if you cannot reach something.

- Tie back long hair or wear a hat.

- Don't wear loose clothes. Roll up long **sleeves**.

- Keep a fire extinguisher in the cooking area.

Cooking Basics

Before you start...

- Get **permission** from an adult.

- Wash your hands.

- Read the recipe at least once.

- Set out all the ingredients and tools you will need.

When you're done...

- Cover food with plastic wrap or aluminum foil. Use **containers** with lids if you have them.

- Wash all of the dishes and **utensils**.

- Put all of the ingredients and tools back where you found them.

- Clean up your work space.

Using the Microwave

- Use microwave-safe dishes.

- Never put aluminum foil or metal in the microwave.

- Start with a short cook time. If it's not enough, cook it some more.

- Use oven mitts when taking things out of the microwave.

- Stop the microwave to stir liquids during heating.

Using the Stovetop

- Turn pot handles away from the burners and the edge of the stove.

- Use the temperature setting in the recipe.

- Use pot holders to handle hot pots and pans.

- Do not leave metal **utensils** in pots.

- Don't put anything except pots and pans on or near the burners.

- Use a timer. Check the food and cook it more if needed.

Using the Oven

- Use the temperature setting in the recipe.

- Preheat the oven while making the recipe.

- Use oven-safe dishes.

- Use pot holders or oven mitts to handle baking sheets and dishes.

- Do not touch oven doors. They can be very hot.

- Set a timer. Check the food and bake it more if needed.

A microwave, stovetop, and oven are very useful for cooking food. But they can be **dangerous** if you are not careful. Always ask an adult for help.

Measuring

Wet Ingredients

Set a measuring cup on the counter. Add the liquid until it reaches the amount you need. Check the measurement from eye level.

Dry Ingredients

Use a spoon to put the dry ingredient in the measuring cup or spoon. Put more than you need in the measuring cup or spoon. Run the back of a dinner knife across the top. This removes the extra.

Moist Ingredients

Moist ingredients are things such as brown sugar and dried fruit. They need to be packed down into the measuring cup. Keep packing until the ingredient reaches the measurement line.

Do You Know This = That?

There are different ways to measure the same amount.

 =

3 teaspoons = 1 tablespoon

 =

4 tablespoons = ¼ cup

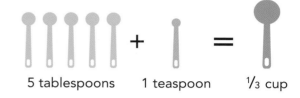

5 tablespoons + 1 teaspoon = ⅓ cup

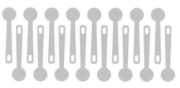 =

16 tablespoons = 1 cup

 =

1 cup = 8 ounces

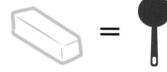

1 stick of butter = ½ cup

2 cups = 1 pint

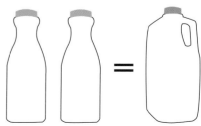

4 cups = 1 quart   2 quarts = ½ gallon

Cooking Terms

Mix

Combine ingredients with a mixing spoon. *Stir* is another word for mix.

Chop

Cut something into very small pieces with a knife.

Whisk

Stir quickly by hand with a whisk or fork.

Boil

Heat liquid until it begins to bubble.

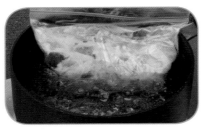

Mash

Crush food until it is soft.

Grate

Shred something into small pieces using a grater.

Melt

Heat something solid until it is softened.

Beat

Stir something with a mixer until it is smooth.

Hard-Boiled Eggs

Preparing

Put the eggs in a pot in a single layer. Add cold water. There should be about 1 inch (3 cm) of water above the eggs. Cover the pot. Heat on high until the water boils. Remove the pot from the heat. Leave the eggs in the pot for 15 minutes. Drain the hot water. Cover the eggs with cold water to cool them.

Peeling

Roll an egg gently on the counter to crack the shell. Hold the egg under running water. Slowly pull off pieces of the shell. Start at the large end. Make sure to remove the thin skin under the shell too. Be careful not to tear the egg white.

Separating the Yolk

To separate an egg, crack it in the middle. Hold it over a bowl. Pull the eggshell apart. Gently pass the egg back and forth between the halves of the shell. The egg white will fall into the bowl. The **yolk** will stay in the shell.

How to Crack an Egg

Tap the egg against the edge of a bowl or counter. Do not hit too hard. Break the shell slightly.

Put your thumbs in the small break. Pull the shell apart. Let the egg drop into a bowl.

Check for pieces of shell in the bowl. If there are any, take them out.

Tools

liquid measuring cup

mixing spoon

sharp knife

fork

cutting board

slotted spoon

medium pot

timer

toaster

hand mixer

tongs

dry measuring cups

measuring spoons

frying pan

12

9 × 13-inch baking dish

large pot

wax paper

oven mitts

spoon

pot holders

spatula

whisk

grater

mixing bowls

quart-size freezer bags

9 × 13-inch
baking sheet

Ingredients

prepared mustard

pizza sauce

non-stick
cooking spray

eggs

seasoned croutons

cream style corn

mozzarella cheese

milk

Dijon mustard

butter

onion

cheddar cheese

bell peppers

English muffins

Swiss cheese

hash browns

mayonnaise

sugar

white vinegar

tomatoes

bread rolls

bacon

paprika

oregano

onion salt

ham

turkey

taco shells

taco seasoning

vanilla extract

almond extract

mint extract

pepper

salt

Roly-Poly Omelet

A healthy and hearty egg meal that tastes great!

Makes 1 serving

ingredients

2 large or extra-large eggs

2 tablespoons cheddar cheese, grated

2 tablespoons ham, chopped

1 tablespoon onion, chopped

1 tablespoon bell pepper, chopped

1 tablespoon tomato, chopped

½ cup hash browns, cooked

tools

grater

frying pan

sharp knife

cutting board

quart-size plastic freezer bag

measuring spoons

measuring cups

medium pot

slotted spoon or tongs

pot holders

timer

1 Crack the eggs into the freezer bag. Seal the bag. Make sure to get all of the air out. Gently **squeeze** the bag to mix the eggs together.

2 Add the other ingredients to the bag. Squeeze to mix well.

3 Boil water in a medium pot. Turn the heat to medium-high. Put the bag in the boiling water for 13 minutes.

4 Remove the bag with the slotted spoon or tongs. Carefully open the bag. Tip the omelet onto a plate.

TIP: It is important to use freezer bags. They are made of heavier plastic than regular bags.

Ahoy Mate! Egg Boats

Sail straight for great taste with this snack!

Makes 24 servings

ingredients

12 hard-boiled eggs, peeled
 and cut in half lengthwise
2 teaspoons Dijon mustard
2 teaspoons white vinegar
⅓ cup mayonnaise
2 bell peppers, washed
paprika

tools

medium mixing bowl
fork
measuring spoons
measuring cups
sharp knife
cutting board
ruler
spoon
large pot

1. Remove the egg **yolks**. Put them in a bowl. Mash them with a fork.

2. Add the mustard and vinegar. Mix in the mayonnaise. Stir until smooth.

3. Cut the peppers into strips. They should be 1 inch (3 cm) wide. Cut the strips into 1-inch (3 cm) squares. Cut each square in half to make triangles.

4. Fill the egg-white halves with the yolk mixture. Put a pepper sail on top of each one. Sprinkle them with paprika.

TIP: For how to cook and peel hard-boiled eggs, see page 11.

Muy Bueno Egg Tacos

Try these for a south-of-the-border meal anytime!

Makes 4 tacos

ingredients

4 taco shells

non-stick cooking spray

4 hard-boiled eggs, peeled
  and chopped

½ cup canned cream style
  corn

1 teaspoon taco seasoning

½ cup cheddar cheese, grated

tools

grater

sharp knife

cutting board

small frying pan

measuring cups

measuring spoons

mixing spoon

pot holders

timer

1 Warm the taco shells according to the instructions on the package.

2 Cover the frying pan lightly with cooking spray. Mix the eggs, corn, and taco seasoning in the pan. Cook on medium heat for 3 minutes. Stir often.

3 Put the pan on a pot holder. Stir in half of the cheese.

4 Put some of the mixture in each taco shell. Sprinkle the rest of the cheese over the tacos.

TIP: For how to cook and peel hard-boiled eggs, see page 11.

Egg-cellent Pizza Pie

An Italian delight for breakfast, lunch, or dinner!

Makes 4 servings

ingredients

6 eggs
½ teaspoon salt
¼ teaspoon oregano
pepper
1 tablespoon butter
¼ cup pizza sauce
½ cup mozzarella cheese,
    grated

tools

grater
measuring cups & spoons
medium mixing bowl
fork
frying pan
spatula
pot holders
sharp knife
cutting board
timer

1. Put the eggs, salt, oregano, and a **dash** of pepper in a bowl. Add ⅓ cup water. Whisk with a fork.

2. Melt the butter in the pan on medium heat. Add the egg mixture.

3. Wait for the eggs to start cooking. Lift the edges to let the uncooked mixture get underneath. Continue until the eggs are completely cooked.

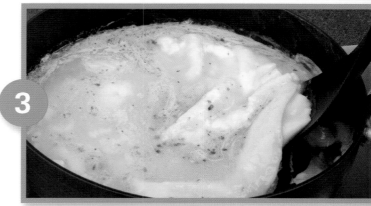

4. Pour the pizza sauce evenly over the cooked eggs. Sprinkle the cheese on top.

5. Put the pan on a pot holder. Cover the pan. Let it sit for 2 minutes to melt the cheese.

6. Push the eggs from the pan onto a cutting board. Cut it into four slices.

Eggy Muffin Melts

Make yummy, eggy breakfast sandwiches!

Makes 4 servings

ingredients

2 English muffins, toasted
1 teaspoon butter
4 eggs
2 tablespoons milk
½ teaspoon salt
8 slices ham or turkey
½ cup cheddar cheese, grated
paprika

tools

grater
toaster
measuring spoons & cups
frying pan
medium mixing bowl
whisk
mixing spoon
pot holders
9 × 13-inch baking sheet
timer

1 Melt the butter in the pan on medium heat. Whisk the eggs, milk, and salt together in a bowl. Pour the egg mixture into the pan.

2 Stir eggs until scrambled. Put the pan on a pot holder.

3 Put the muffin halves on the baking sheet. Put two meat slices on each muffin half. Spoon eggs on top. Sprinkle with cheese and paprika.

4 Broil the muffins for 1 to 2 minutes until the cheese begins to bubble.

TIP: To broil, move the oven rack up as high as possible. Use the broil oven setting. Keep the door open slightly. Make sure the food does not burn.

Egg Bowl Supreme

An awesome egg meal cooked in a bread roll!

Makes 4 servings

ingredients

4 bread rolls
4 large eggs
4 slices bacon, cooked
4 tablespoons Swiss cheese, grated

tools

grater
frying pan
tongs
sharp knife
cutting board
measuring spoons
9 × 13-inch baking sheet
oven mitts
timer

1. Preheat the oven to 350 **degrees**. Cut ½ inch (1 cm) off the top of each roll.

2. Use your fingers to remove the insides of the rolls.

3. Crack an egg into each roll. Put a slice of bacon and 1 tablespoon cheese on each roll.

4. Put the rolls on the baking sheet. Bake for 20 minutes.

5. Put the top on each roll. Bake for 5 more minutes.

Egg 'n Stuff Casserole

A hot dish for special occasions that everyone will love!

Makes 8 servings

ingredients

non-stick cooking spray

2 cups seasoned croutons

1 cup cheddar cheese, grated

4 ounces ham, chopped

8 eggs

2 cups milk

½ teaspoon salt

½ teaspoon prepared mustard

⅛ teaspoon onion salt

pepper

tools

grater

9 × 13-inch glass baking dish

measuring cups & spoons

sharp knife

cutting board

oven mitts

whisk

medium mixing bowl

timer

1 Preheat the oven to 325 **degrees**.

2 Cover the baking dish lightly with cooking spray. Put the croutons in the bottom. Put the cheese on top of the croutons. Put the ham on top of the cheese.

3 Put the eggs, milk, salt, mustard, onion salt, and a **dash** of pepper in a bowl. Whisk them together.

4 Pour the egg mixture over the ingredients in the baking dish.

5 Bake for 60 to 65 minutes.

Marvy Meringues

A sweet egg treat that melts in your mouth!

Makes 12 meringues

ingredients
3 large egg whites, no yolks
(see page 11)

salt

mint, almond, or vanilla
extract flavoring

¾ cups sugar

tools
large mixing bowl

hand mixer

measuring cups & spoons

9 × 13-inch baking sheet

wax paper

spoon

oven mitts

timer

1   Preheat the oven to 300 **degrees**.

2   Put egg whites, a **pinch** of salt, and a **dash** of flavoring in a bowl. Beat for 1 minute on low speed. Set mixer on medium speed. Beat for 2 to 3 minutes. The mixture should be **fluffy**.

3   Set the mixer on high speed. Add the sugar one tablespoon at a time. Beat it until the mixture is stiff and shiny.

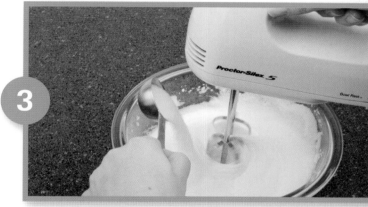

4   Cover the baking sheet with wax paper. Drop heaping spoonfuls of the egg mixture onto the wax paper.

5   Bake for 30 to 40 minutes or until they look pale and dry. Turn the oven off. Leave the meringues in the oven to cool.

Glossary

container – something that other things can be put into.

dangerous – able or likely to cause harm or injury.

dash – a very small amount added with a quick, downward shake.

degree – the unit used to measure temperature.

fluffy – light, soft, and airy.

mineral – a natural element that plants, animals, and people need to be healthy.

permission – when a person in charge says it's okay to do something.

pinch – the amount you can hold between your thumb and one finger.

protein – a substance needed for good health, found naturally in meat, eggs, beans, nuts, and milk.

sleeve – the part of a piece of clothing that covers some or all of the arm.

squeeze – to press or grip something tightly.

utensil – a tool used to prepare or eat food.

vitamin – a substance needed for good health, found naturally in plants and meats.

yolk – the yellow part inside an egg.